A DUCK'S EYE VIEW OF
BOSTON

Demetri and Mina Papoulidis

Charles River, John Hancock Tower
The Charles River separates Boston
from Cambridge and Charlestown.
Hundreds of ducks call the "Charles"
their home.

Copyright © 2008 by
Demetri & Mina X. Papoulidis

Published by
Demetri Productions LLC
Arlington, Massachusetts

© Photography by
Demetri & Mina X. Papoulidis

First Published 2009

Printed and bound in China
ISBN 13: 978-0-615-18487-6

For more information about this book,
please visit:

www.duckseyeview.com

Photography, Design and Text by
Demetri Papoulidis and
Mina Xanthopoulos Papoulidis

Charles River

Sailing on the Charles River is
a favorite summer past-time.

INTRODUCTION:

A Duck's Eye View of Boston

What better way to view this
picturesque city than through the
eyes of Boston's beloved ducks.
They can be found swimming on
the Charles River, the waterfront
and around the pond in the
Public Garden. You can even let a
"Duck" give you a tour of the city
by catching a ride on the popular
Boston Duck Tours. If you need a
break, sit back, relax and enjoy a
scenic cruise around the pond on
the Public Garden's majestic swan
boats; not really ducks but close
in relation. While in the Garden
be sure to view the famous bronze
sculpture of a happy family of
ducks waddling by. Needless to
say, the duck has become Boston's
unofficial mascot.

Most of the photographs in this
book capture Boston in an 180
degree panoramic angle. This
global view is our perception of
how a duck sees the world. By
photographing the city with our
special lens we are able to frame
more things in one shot resulting
in an original perspective. This
artistic view of Boston truly
remains a one-of-a kind "Duck's
Eye View".

right
**Aerial View of the Financial District
and the Waterfront**

4

Charles River from Cambridge
Walking along the banks of the "Charles" you can view the city skyline and catch a glimpse of a family of ducks swimming by.

Beacon Hill
Gas lanterns and decorative iron-work accent the desirable Beacon Hill neighborhood.

Beacon Hill
The charming façades of shops, galleries, restaurants and cafes are found along the quaint brick streets of Beacon Hill.

Beacon Street
Tinted purple glass windows are found on older Beacon Hill homes. This unique effect was caused by defective glass that turned purple once exposed to sunlight.

Beacon Hill Neighborhood

The beautiful residential neighborhood of Beacon Hill is characterized by its old world colonial charm. These historic homes are mostly designed in Greek Revival, Federal, and Victorian period architecture.

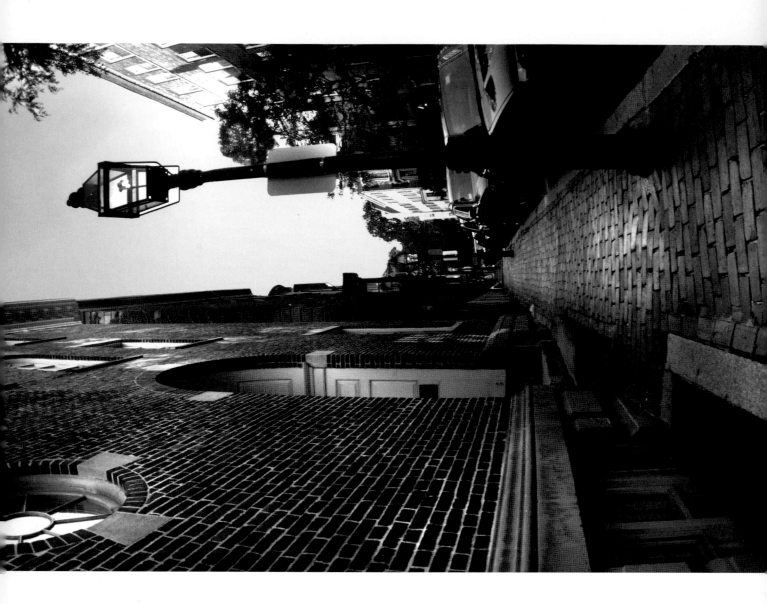

Brick Row Houses on Beacon Hill

The Museum of Fine Arts

Boston's Museum of Fine Arts' exquisite galleries showcase over one million objects. The museum was established in 1876 and is well-known for its French Impressionist collection.

Native American Statue

The Native American statue standing at the entrance of the Museum represents Cyrus Dallin's "Appeal to the Great Spirit". It was completed in 1909.

18

above

A Picturesque View of the Esplanade from a Footbridge

left

Hatch Shell

This 40-foot high band shell was built in 1940 in memory of Edward Hatch. The Hatch shell sits on a two-acre lawn along the "Charles" where people gather to revel in a variety of cultural shows. Every 4th of July the Boston Pops Orchestra performs under a dazzling display of fireworks.

opposite

Arthur Fiedler Statue

Located on the Esplanade near the Hatch Shell this statue is of the nationally renowned maestro Arthur Fiedler; the longest-serving maestro of the Boston Pops.

19

A Path Along the Esplanade
The Esplanade's unique landscape
stretches out seventeen miles along
the Charles River.

John Joseph Moakley Courthouse
The modern structure of the court-
house is located along the Boston
Harbor.

USS Constitution
Nicknamed "Old Ironsides", the USS Constitution was built in 1797 and is the oldest commissioned warship afloat in the world. The ship is located in Charlestown.

above
Fountain at Copley Square

opposite
Copley Square
Copley Square is the core of the Back Bay. Magnificent sights of Trinity Church, the John Hancock Tower and the Boston Public Library can be viewed from Copley Square Plaza.

below
Rabbit Sculpture
Located in Copley Square, Nancy Schön's bronze sculpture of the "Tortoise and the Hare" honors the runners of the annual Boston Marathon.

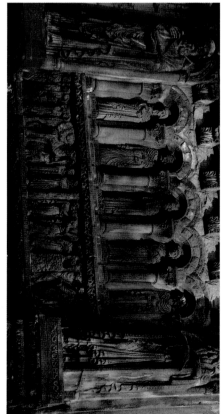

Trinity Church
Designed by Henry Hobson Richardson and completed in 1877, this Romanesque style church is one of America's finest architectural buildings.

27

above
Arlington Street Church
Arlington Street Church, built in 1861, was the first public building in Boston's Back Bay.

right
Arlington Church steeple
The church has a set of 16 steeple bells that are rung by hand.

left and overleaf
Newbury Street
Enjoy upscale shopping, fine
art galleries and leisure dining
housed in 19th century townhouses.

Brewer Fountain
This bronze fountain by Paul Lienard is located on the Boston Common. It is a replica of the award winning French original and was donated by Gardner Brewer in 1868.

John Hancock Tower
Designed by I.M. Pei in 1976, the John
Hancock tower is the tallest building
in New England. The "mirrored" glass
exterior reflects the historical buildings
in Copley Square.

Faneuil Hall Marketplace
Strolling along the cobblestone streets of Faneuil Hall Marketplace you will discover an array of unique shops, restaurants and cafes. Special events and creative street performances contribute to the colorful atmosphere.

opposite
Rowes Wharf
Rowes Wharf, located in Boston's historic waterfront district, features luxury hotels and impressive waterfront views.

left
Aerial View of Old South Church

above detail
Old South Church Entrance

opposite
Old South Church
Built in 1875, Old South Church's
majestic Italian Gothic architecture
portrays old world elegance.

Symphony Hall
Boston Symphony Hall is one of the top concert halls in the world. Wallace Clement Sabine, a physics professor at Harvard developed a mathematical formula enabling superb acoustics to be heard throughout the concert hall. Leaving audiences with a remarkably memorable experience.

38

Harvard University

Harvard University was founded in 1636 and is the oldest university in the United States. This Ivy League school is one of the top academic institutions in the world. Inside the Harvard Yard gates are 25-acres of grassy campus and ivy covered buildings.

Widener Library
Widener Library is one of Harvard's best-known buildings where students can meet to study and socialize.

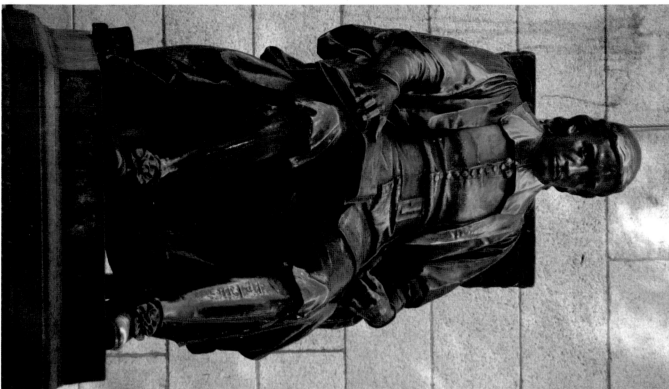

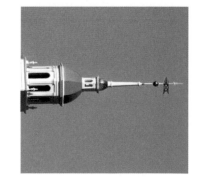

far left
John Harvard Statue
The John Harvard statue, completed in 1884 by Daniel Chester French, is located in front of University Hall. Legend says that by rubbing the statue's shoe you will come into good luck.

left and above detail
Harvard University Steeples
The many steeples of the university are visible form all around Harvard Square.

Harvard Yard

left
Harvard Law School

above right
Entering into Harvard Yard

below right detail
**A Clock on the Façade of a
Harvard Building Overlooking
Harvard Square**

above
Chess in Harvard Square
For a fair price you can play a challenging game of chess with one of Harvard Square's Chess Masters.

above right
The Harvard Coop
Located in the heart of Harvard Square, the Harvard Coop was founded by a group of students in 1882 as a cooperative society to sell affordable merchandise to the Harvard community.

above
Out of Town News
This extraordinary newsstand carries hard to find publications, including a wide selection of foreign magazines.

right
Curious George
The whimsical entrance of this famous children's book and toy store in Harvard Square beckons you to come inside and explore.

opposite below right
Harvard Square
Harvard Square is a mecca for talented street musicians and artists.

"Make Way for Ducklings" Statue
Nancy Schön's adorable ducklings and their mother, Mrs. Mallard, is a popular site in the Public Garden. The bronze statues were inspired by the children's picture book "Make Way for Ducklings" by Robert McCloskey.

A Cold Winter's Day
Red scarfs keep Mrs. Mallard and her
eight Ducklings: Jack, Kack, Lack,
Mack, Nack, Ouack, Pack and Quack
warm in the winter.

above
Storrow Drive
A gondola glides on the Charles River along Storrow Drive.

opposite
Ray and Maria Stata Center at Massachusetts Institute of Technology
This unusually notable architectural structure was designed by renowned architect Frank O. Gehry for the Computer, Information and Intelligence Sciences.

48

Berklee College of Music
Berklee was founded in 1945 and is the world's largest independent music college. Berklee prides itself on its Grammy nominated and winning alumni and faculty.

a b o v e
Architectural Detail of Berklee College of Music

50

Boston University
Students lounge on the grassy
Boston University city campus.

51

left and above right detail

Cheers

Located in Beacon Hill, Cheers was originally named Bull & Finch Pub. This neighborhood bar was the inspiration for the hit television show "Cheers".

opposite

View from Copley Square

The "mirrored" glass of the John Hancock Tower reflects Trinity Church and a "Duck Tour" passing by.

above
Aerial View of the Back Bay
The prestigious Back Bay neighborhood is known for its quaint brownstones.

opposite
Chinatown Gate
Upon entering this elaborately decorative gate you are immediately immersed in Asian culture. Authentic restaurants, bakeries, teahouses and colorful characters painted on shop windows are found throughout the busy streets of Chinatown.

54

Old Granary Burying Ground
Founded in 1660, the Granary is the third oldest burying ground in Boston. Notable graves include Patriots John Hancock, Samuel Adams and Robert Treat Paine. Also buried here are the victims of the Boston Massacre and the wife of Isaac Vergoose, who is believed to be "Mother Goose", author of the famous nursery rhymes.

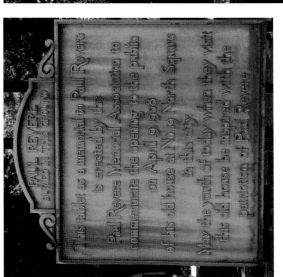

PAUL REVERE
BURIED IN THIS GROUND

This tablet as a memorial to Paul Revere
is erected by the
Paul Revere Memorial Association to
commemorate the opening to the public
on April 19, 1908
of his old house at No. 19 North Square
in this city
May the youth of today when they visit
this old house be inspired with the
patriotism of Paul Revere

FRANKLIN

King's Chapel Burying Ground
As the oldest burying place in Boston this burying ground is the final resting place for many colonists, including Governor John Winthrop and Mary Chilton; the first woman to step off the Mayflower in 1620.

above detail, right and far right
Irish Famine Memorial
These bronze statues are a tribute to
the catastrophic famine that took place
in Ireland from 1845-1850.

below
Old South Meeting Hall
Here is the site where protest meetings
were held that led to the infamous
Boston Tea Party. Built in 1729, it
was the largest building in Colonial
Boston.

opposite
Omni Parker House
The Omni Parker House is located in
downtown Boston on the Freedom
Trail. Opened in 1855, it is the longest
running luxury hotel in America.

opposite
Massachusetts Institute of Technology
MIT is located on 168 acres that extend
more than a mile along the Cambridge
side of the Charles River. The Institute
admitted its first students in 1865. Today MIT is a world-class teaching and
research institution.

left
**Classic Greek Columns Mark the
Entrance of MIT**

above detail
**Decorative Motif Located above the
Entrance**

Longfellow Bridge

The Longfellow Bridge is named after the American poet Henry Wadsworth Longfellow whose famous works include "Paul Revere's Ride". Originally known as the Cambridge Bridge, it was the first major route across the Charles River.

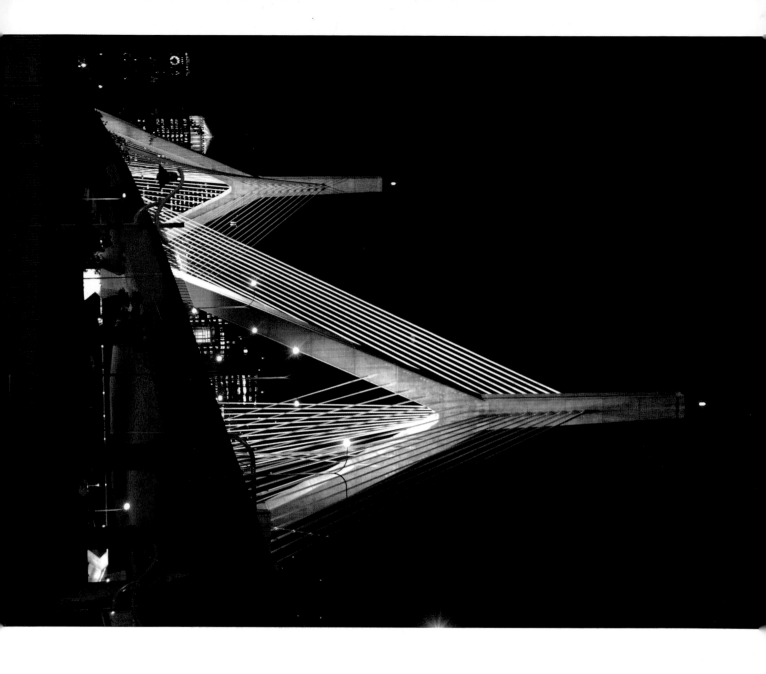

Leonard P. Zakim Bunker Hill Bridge

This 10-lane cable-stayed bridge is the widest cable-stayed bridge in the world. With 30-story towers, it was designed to mimic the Bunker Hill Monument. The bridge is named after civil rights activist Lenny Zakim (1953-1999). He was the New England Director of the Anti-Defamation.

opposite
Christmas Time in Faneuil Hall Marketplace
An enormous Christmas tree in the center of Faneuil Hall Marketplace spreads holiday spirit.

above and below right
Faneuil Hall Marketplace
Tourists and locals frequent this bustling marketplace for its amusing street performers, unique shopping and scrumptious dining experiences.

above right
Custom House Tower
The Custom House Tower is located in the Financial District. During the mid-19th century this 496 foot tower was the tallest building in Boston.

Boston Common
Birds take flight on the Boston Common on a snowy day.

Boston Common, Beacon Hill
The brick row houses viewed
from the Boston Common
illustrate a striking contrast
against the newly fallen snow.

right
Quincy Hall Market Building
Built in 1822, this 500 foot long granite two-story building is topped with an impressive copper dome in the center. It was once a major fish and meat market. Today it houses a wide selection of eateries and unique gift shops and pushcarts.

below details
Faneuil Hall Marketplace Attractions
Whether you are strolling along the stoned cobbled streets, shopping, or just sitting at an outdoor café, the original architecture of Faneuil Hall Marketplace will transport you back to Colonial Boston.

left
Faneuil Hall Building
Built in 1742 in the style of an old English country market, the Faneuil Hall Building became a gathering place to hear political speeches. A statue of the politician Samuel Adams, whose speeches where quite rebellious, stands proudly in front of the building.

below left
The Freedom Trail
Paved with red bricks, this 2.5 mile walking trail leads you along many important historical sites.

below right
Bell in Hand Tavern
Enjoy a lager in America's oldest running tavern; opened in 1795.

Old State House
Built in 1713, this is the oldest public building in Boston. It once was the Massachusetts Bay Colony government office headquarters. Today it is a museum where you can view early Boston history.

South Station

South Station is located at the intersection of Atlantic Avenue and Summer Street in Dewey Square; it is the largest train station in Boston.

Holocaust Memorial
Millions of prisoners' numbers
are etched on the six towers
which represent the six death
camps of World War II.

Entrance to the Public Garden

A wrought-iron gate leads to 24-acres of colorful Victorian flower beds, enchanting weeping willows, a tranquil pond and a variety of bronze sculptures. Also inhabiting the garden are ducks, swans, birds and butterflies.

Boston Public Garden

Established in 1837, the Boston Public Garden is located in the heart of the city and was the first public botanical garden in America.

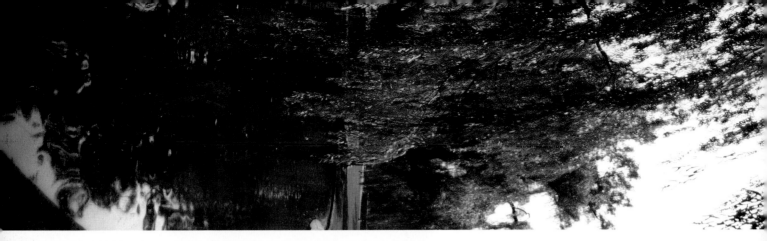

Views of the Public Garden

opposite
Under a Weeping Willow
The Boston Public Garden offers
tranquil refuge from busy city life.

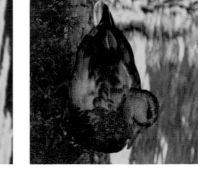

above right and opposite
Bridge Over the Pond
A suspension bridge in the Garden's center is said to be the smallest suspension bridge in the world.

below right
Sculpture of a Young Boy
Whimsical sculptures of children are scattered throughout the Public Garden.

below far right
A Colorful Flower Bed
Winding paths lead to many surprises in the Public Garden.

right
**George Robert White Memorial,
"The Spirit of Giving"**
This bronze angel by Daniel Chester French stands majestically in the Public Garden. Beacon Hill townhouses appear in the background.

left
Statue of Colonel William Prescott
Colonel William Prescott led the rebel forces in the battle of Bunker Hill.

opposite
Bunker Hill Monument
Bunker Hill in Charlestown was the site of the first major battle of the American Revolution on June 17, 1775. Standing at 221 feet tall, the Bunker Hill Monument is made entirely of granite.

The Boston Skyline at Night

opposite
Old City Hall

This building was occupied as Boston City Hall from 1865–1969. The noble white granite exterior framed with decorative columns is designed in the French Second Empire style.

above
George Washington Equestrian Statue

A little past the entrance of the Public Garden stands a grand equestrian of George Washington. Created by Thomas Ball in 1869, this statue reflects the post civil war era.

Museum of Science

above left
Hood Milk Bottle
A giant Hood milk bottle serves as an ice cream stand which landmarks the Children's Museum.

above right
Museum of Science
A huge Tyrannosaurus Rex invites you into the Museum of Science.

below
Children's Museum
Children and parents have fun exploring the hands-on exhibits.

opposite
South Boston
A large deck overlooks the Boston Harbor and the Fort Point Channel.

North End

The North End is an Italian neighbor-hood in Boston; it is popular for its many restaurants and cafes that offer mouth-watering authentic Italian delicacies.

In summertime this quaint neighbor-hood hosts large spirited festivals commemorating various Catholic Saints.

Saint Stephen's Roman Catholic Church
Handsomely bold in style, Saint Stephen's is located in the heart of Boston's "Little Italy" in the North End. Built in 1714, it was designed by the famous Boston architect Charles Bulfinch.

Equestrian of Paul Revere
A popular site to see in the North End is Cyrus Dallin's bronze statue of Paul Revere. Dallin depicts a physically strong Paul Revere on his famous ride.

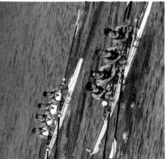

Charles Regatta
Spectators gather along the Charles River to cheer on athletes participating in the Charles Regatta. This is an annual world famous two-day competitive rowing event that takes place in the fall.

Head of the Charles Regatta
Athletes compete for the winning
title "Head of the Charles".

overleaf
Leonard P. Zakim Bunker Hill Bridge
This view is from the banks of the
Charles River in Cambridge.

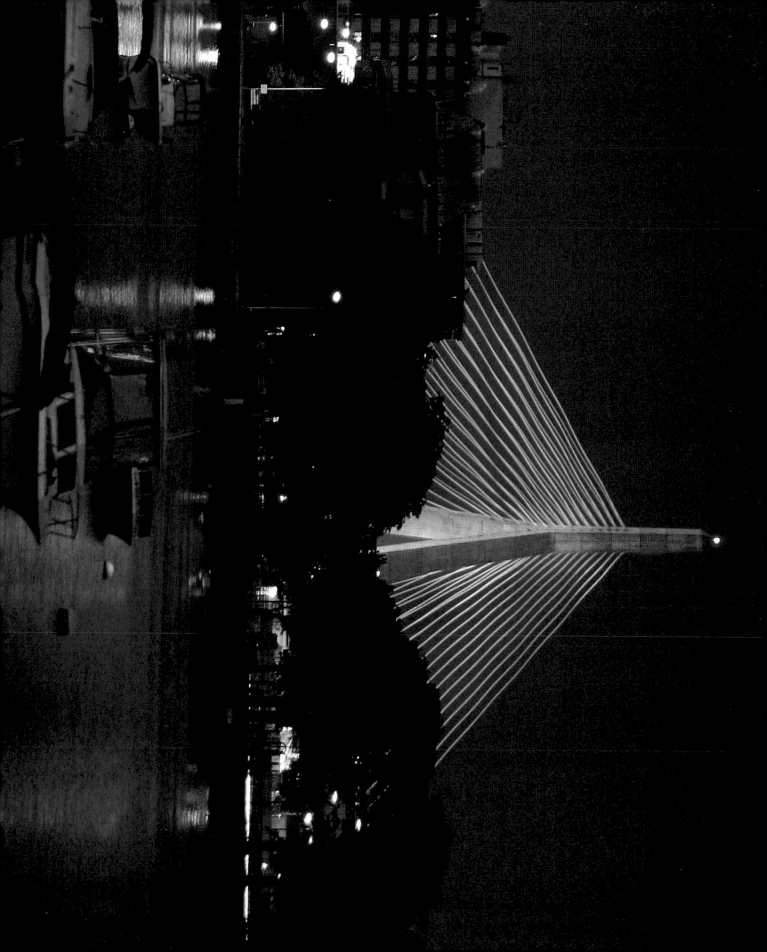

Financial District
This thriving section of town is home to many businesses, luxury hotels, trendy restaurants and nightclubs.

Fenway Park
Home of the Boston Red
Sox, Fenway Park is the
oldest occupied Major
League Baseball stadium
in the country.

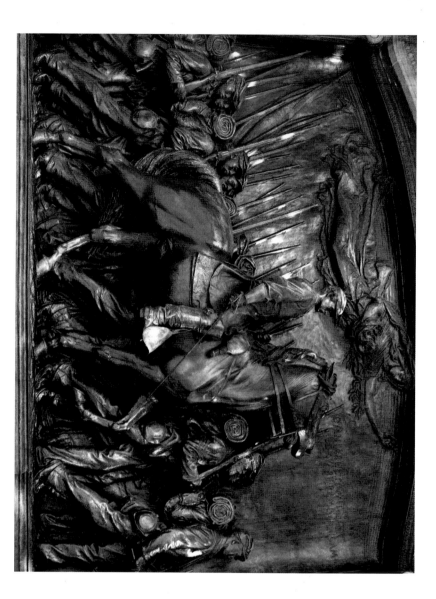

above

Shaw Memorial

A bronze sculpture that is located
across from the State House depicts
Colonel Robert Gould Shaw and the
54th Regiment.

opposite

Frog Pond

On a hot summer's day the Frog Pond
on the Boston Common beckons you
to splash around and cool off. In the
winter the pond transforms into an
ice-skating rink for a picturesque place
to skate.

above right

**The Statue of "America", Soldiers'
and Sailors' Monument**

Located on Flagstaff Hill in the Boston
Common is the Soldiers' and Sailors'
Monument. Standing tall on top of
this huge monument is the statue of
"America". This bronze statue is of a
dominant female dressed in classic
Greek costume and crowned with
thirteen stars.

below

Soldiers' and Sailors' Monument

Proud patriotic female figures deco-
rate the column of the Soldiers'
and Sailors' Monument.

Snow Blankets the Boston Common

Prudential Center

The Prudential Center is one of Boston's top shopping and dining spots. Enjoy panoramic views of the city from the "Skywalk Observatory" and from the stylish restaurant "Top of the Hub".

104

above
Aerial View of the Prudential Center

right
View of the Prudential Tower from the Christian Science Center

left
Detail of the Prudential Tower

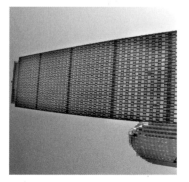

above
Inside of the Prudential Center Mall

right
Prudential Plaza Bronze Sculpture
This dynamic athletic figure appears to be reaching up towards the Prudential Tower.

107

The Christian Science Center
The Christian Science Center occupies an entire city block. Significant buildings can be viewed here such as: the original Mother Church (1894); the larger extension (1906) and I.M. Pei's modern plaza and reflecting pool (1968-74).

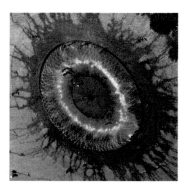

Old Northern Avenue Footbridge
This bridge allows you to cross over to South Boston by foot.

Leonard P. Zakim Bunker Hill Bridge
View from Charlestown

Massachusetts State House
The State House is located on top of Beacon Hill overlooking the Boston Common. It was built in the stately Federal style by architect Charles Bulfinch, 1795-1797. The glittering 23-carat gold dome can be seen throughout the area.

Entrance to the Boston Common

Stone stairs leading to the Boston Common are aligned with old fashioned street lamps and detailed wrought-iron railings.

above
Commercial Wharf
This scenic seaport is situated in downtown Boston's historic waterfront.

below right
Christopher Columbus Waterfront Park
Besides featuring the best views of the Boston Harbor, this park has a fountain for splashing, a rose garden for leisurely walks and a vast grassy area for picnics.

below far right
Christopher Columbus Statue
Located in Christopher Columbus Park this statue recognizes Italian contributions to Boston's heritage.

opposite
The Financial District

Boston Harbor Hotel
The luxurious Boston Harbor Hotel's grand archway with its beautiful gold-domed rotunda, leads to the scenic Harbor.

above
Brick Row Houses on Beacon Hill

right
The Boston Common
The Boston Common with views of the
city.

far left
Old North Church
Located in the North End neighbor-hood and built in 1723, the Old North Church is the oldest church in Boston. Since the steeple can be easily viewed from across the Charles River, it was an important landmark during the American Revolution.

left
Park Street Church
Built in 1809, the Park Street Church has an impressive 217 foot steeple.

above detail
Detail of the Park Street Church

Boston Public Library
Built in 1848, this was the first
library in America. The library's

Italian Renaissance architecture
contributes to the old world charm
of Copley Square.

120

Gazebo in the snow
An alluring white stone gazebo blends in perfectly with the newly fallen snow on the Boston Common.

above detail
View of the Zakim Bridge from Charlestown

right
Boston Skyline at Night, Charlestown
Striking views of the Boston skyline can be observed from Charlestown.

Swan Boats, Public Garden
The uniquely designed foot-propelled Swan Boats in the pond of the Public Garden are the only boats of their kind in the world.

124

John Hancock Tower
In this aerial view, the John Hancock Tower dominates the Back Bay area.

Detail of the John Hancock Tower

right
Panoramic View of the Back Bay

Boston has several famous nicknames including "Beantown", "The Hub" and "The Walking City". Beantown comes from the popular colonial dish that was widely served in the city; baked beans and molasses. The "Hub" was created by the witty Bostonian writer and poet Oliver Wendell Holmes, it refers to Boston being the Hub of the Universe. "The Walking City" is derived from Boston's 17th century planning. Meant for horse and buggy travel, the confusing labyrinth of narrow winding one-way streets has not changed much since colonial times. Walking and using Boston's efficient public transportation system is the ideal way to enjoy this picturesque city.

126

above
Commonwealth Avenue
A jogger on a snowy day demonstrates that true Bostonians are not affected by the weather.

About the Authors
Only true Bostonians can depict the city as profoundly as Demetri and Mina Papoulidis. Living in Boston their entire lives, this artistic couple portray their home city not only through patriotic eyes, but they push creative boundaries to present to the public a book of Boston that is beyond the ordinary. As professional photographers they are well-known for their artistic photojournalistic wedding photography, portraiture and landscapes. Through artistic framing and creative lighting they constantly challenge themselves to capture the mundane in extraordinary ways.